The Soul of an Island

The Soul of an Island

Photographs and writings by Mimi Merton

White Caps Press
Nantucket

Photographs and text Copyright (c) 1999 by Mimi Merton

All rights reserved. No part of the contents of this book may be used or reproduced in any form without written permission from the publisher.

Printed in China
9 8 7 6 5 4 3 2

Library of Congress Card Number: 99-91257

ISBN 0-9675239-7-4

Published and distributed by
White Caps Press
4 Quince Street
Nantucket, Massachusetts 02554

www.whitecapspress.com

for Marc and Chris

With thanks to Walter Lucas, Ron Lynch and Bruce Marshall-Jones for their guidance. And to my family and friends, who have given me love, encouragement and support, always.

Dedicated to my father

The Soul of an Island

The Soul of an Island

The soul of an island

is the cry of a gull.

It is the waves crashing upon the shore.

It is the sweet fragrance of roses

melting into the soft summer air.

It is that place

where the sea meets the sky,

where each of us become one...

where life is

forgiving.

The Sea

There is something reassuring

about the sea...

about the constancy it possesses.

To know that the tide

will always come in

and always recede again.

To hear the rhythm of its voice

in the cool night air

and know that in the morning

it will still be there,

there is something reassuring

about the sea...

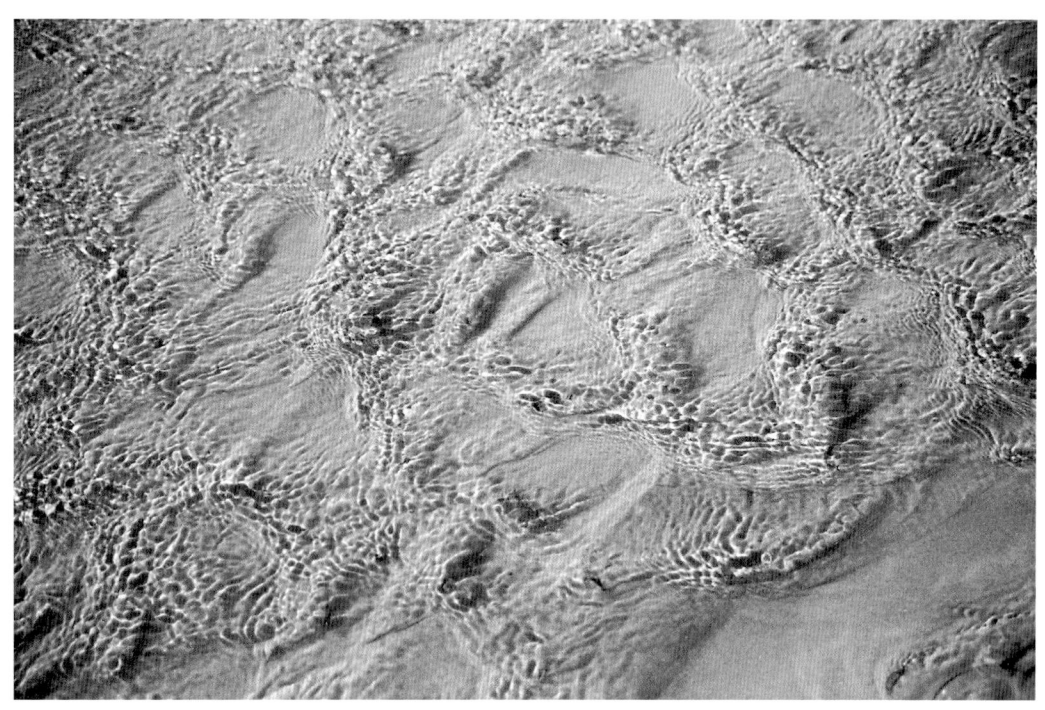

Grey Lady

She is a soft breeze

blowing

through beach grass

on a dune.

Church bells and cherry blossoms,

early morning fog horns…

summer winds, autumn moors

the quietness of snow.

Cradled by the sea

and warmed by the sun,

Nantucket is a gift

to be treasured.

Morning

Snowflakes fall

out of a pale grey sky

dancing

to the gentle music

of the morning.

For a brief moment in time

their carefree journey

leads them

downward, filling the air

with magic.

Then suddenly they disappear.

The sky turns blue,

the dance is over...

and sunflakes brighten

the brand new day.

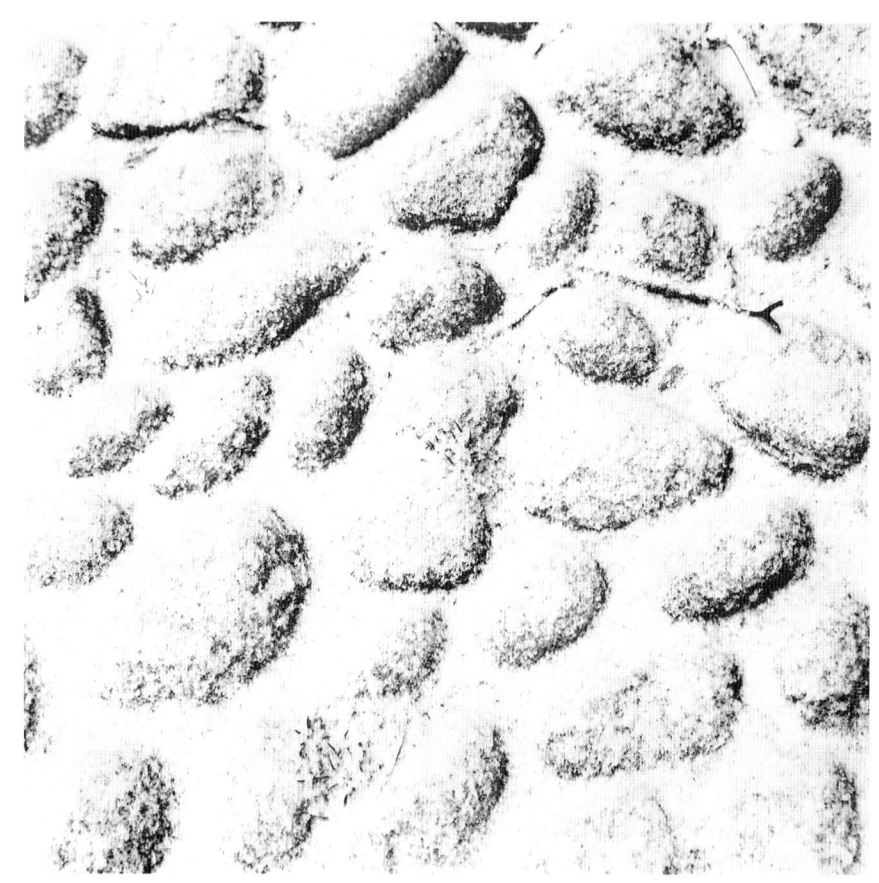

Awakening

A new day is born

into the orange glow

of morning. We are given

the first day of Spring.

Birds chatter

in the trees

and the breeze whispers

softly.

The music

of this day

has

begun.

Fog

Soft and grey...

it whispers

across the morning.

Ghostly images linger,

the Brant Point beacon calls

in the distance.

Time has stopped...

the world is far away.

Lily Pond

Early morning walk.

Much of the world still sleeps.

I drift from the pavement

and feel grass, wet with morning dew

beneath my feet.

With each step

town becomes country.

Birds resound,

rabbits frolic in the grass before me

as if I were not there.

Cattails peer from the reeds

gently swaying in the breeze,

and the old apple tree

crooked with age

bids me good morning.

Autumn

The air is clear.

It is a time of

quieting.

Summer days

have journeyed on...

the island rests in

peaceful beauty.

A Passing Stillness

Sunlight

is peering through

the greyness.

Rain has stopped

but the fog lingers on.

Soon the sun

will chase it away,

bright skies will appear...

and the silence will be

broken.

November

Leaves are falling.

Like a gentle rain

they release their hold

on the old elm tree

and float to the ground,

one by one.

I hear them land,

the tiniest of whispers.

There, they will sleep

to blanket the flowers

from the cold winter snows,

and to be reborn

when the robin sings.

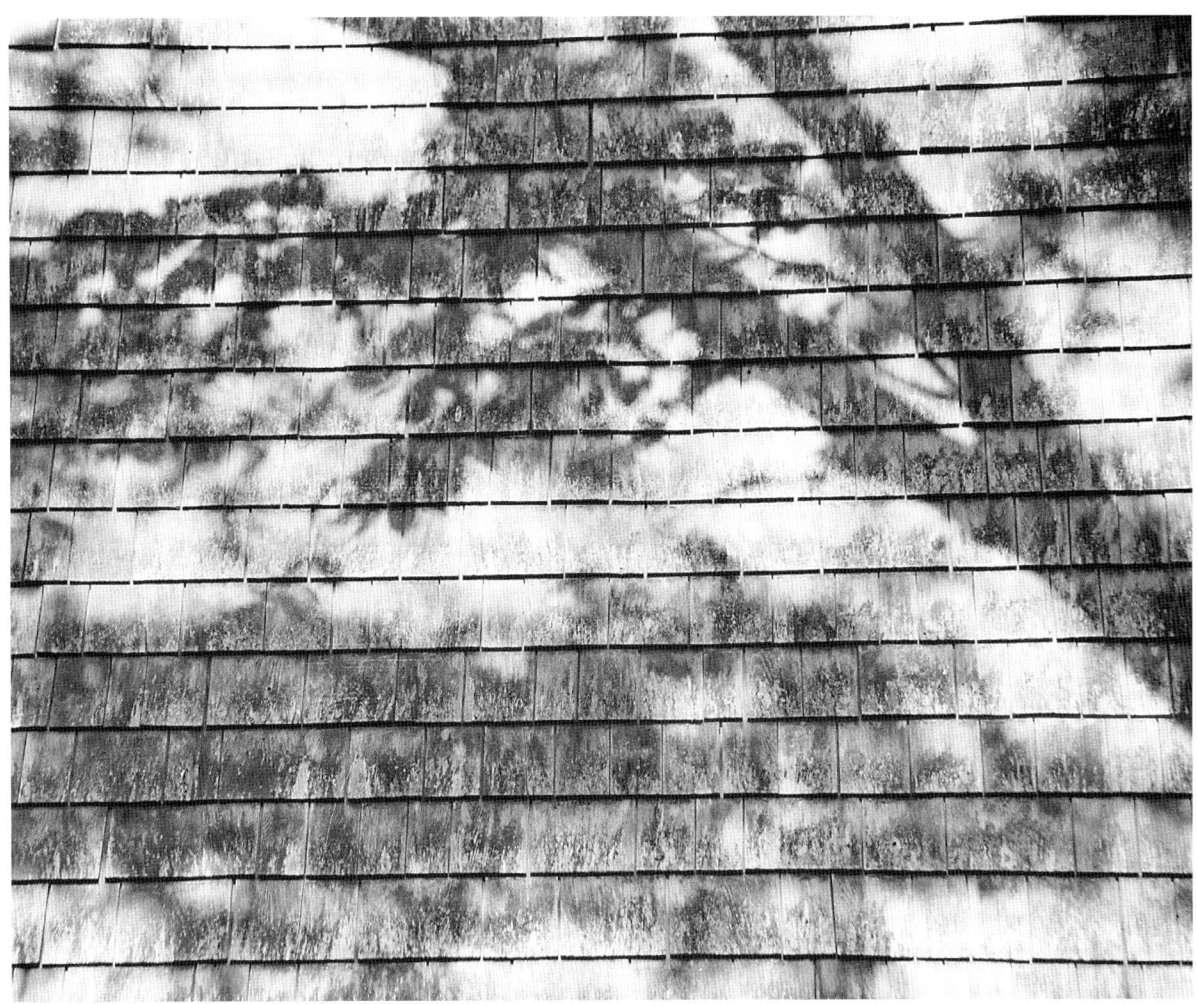

SUSANNA
Daughter of
Paul & Catharine
FOLGER
Died
Nov. 11. 1815.
Æ. 53.

January

Yesterday it snowed...

all day and into the night.

The island closed its doors

and rode out the storm.

This morning she is enshrouded

in a deep blanket of white.

Slowly,

she comes back to life.

A Still, Small Pond

A still, small pond

nestled amongst the moors

lingers

in a reverie.

Mirrored

in cool, dark waters

a hawk soars free

against a pristine sky...

an image

of an unknown time

and the promise of

tomorrows.

Interlude

A pocket of time

hidden from the busy world

where gentle memories

are born.

The silence of peace

the beauty of nature

the warmth of love.

Time away from time.

Sunset at the Point

A bright red sun slips

quietly

into the sea

where seals are playing.

The brand new sliver

of moon

and its solitary star

grace the skies above.

This day has

ended

in a

whisper.

May the soul of this gentle island live on forever

in the hearts of those who care for her.

Author's note:

Thoughts on Home

      I love this island. I love being here. I love that we are surrounded by the sea, that the people here are warm and friendly and outgoing, and that at any given moment I can get emotional just looking at the beauty of nature that surrounds us here.

      Over the years, I have come to know the island intimately. I have walked her moors and beaches, and circumnavigated the island by boat. I have fished her waters and climbed her lighthouses. I have felt the glow of sunset at water's edge, and the softness of the fog that so often envelopes us.

      I love this little faraway island. She is a part of my being. I am so grateful to be here. This is my home.